Essential Oils for Your Dog

Safe Natural Remedies for your Dog or Puppy

(Essential Oils for Dogs, Essential Oils for Puppies, Essential Oils for K9, Natural Dog Care, Natural Remedies for Dogs)

Table of Contents

Introduction

Chapter 1: Essential Oils for Pets: A Summary

Chapter 2: Benefits of Using Essential Oil for your Pets

Chapter 3: Oil Application Techniques for Dogs

Chapter 4: Therapeutic Oil Uses for Dogs

Chapter 5: Insect Repellent Oil Uses for Dogs

Chapter 6: Deodorizing Oil Recipes for Dogs

Chapter 7: Ear Care Oil Recipes for Dogs

Chapter 8: Nose Care Oil Recipes for Dogs

Chapter 9: Skin & Coat Oil Recipes for Dogs

Chapter 10: Flea & Tick Oil Recipes for Dogs

Chapter 11: The Best Online Resources for Essential oil for Dogs

Conclusion

Introduction

The use of essential oils has been a human pastime for centuries – people have been relying on these to cure various ailments, aid in weight loss and boost energy among other things. However have you ever stop to think that essential oils could also be used to enhance the general health of your furry friend? YES, that's right – dogs can also benefits from the wonders of essential oils.

Essential oils give off aromatic smells that harmonize and balance the body while healing it. The principle is simple: the sense of smell takes in the scents which boost inner health which is reflected by heightened physiological functions. This shows how amazing essential oils are in treating a number of health conditions.

This book will help you get a full understanding on how essential oils can be used for your pet dog and the reasons why they should be favored over other forms of treatments. You will learn about the different aspects of essential oils use; in the context of them being used on dogs.

These pages also contain valuable information about the benefits of oils, what types of oils should be used and avoided, methods of application, different treatments associated with essential oils and much more.

As you get more out of this book, you may wish to think about using natural remedies, through oils in order to achieve holistic healing for your dog. If you are a health nut (and that's the likely very reason you are reading this fantastic book) then this guide book is for you!

Essential oils are now integrated to conventional veterinary medicine practices. This is happening because more and more pet owners are becoming more aware on how to use oils to protect and preserve the health of their pets. As a responsible pet owner, you should ensure proper application, to avoid harming your pet in the process. You may also want to consider working with a veterinarian who will not only guide you further in implementing the wide array of treatments in this book, but will also assist you in other concerns, such as diet, and nutritional aspects of your dog.

This book will teach you everything that you need to know to about safely and effectively using essential oils with for your dogs.

So, good luck and I hope you find joy in reading the book!

Chapter 1: Essential Oils for Pets: A Summary

You may be wondering, at this point, what these essential oils are and how they can help. Basically, plants produce oils for various reasons. Some are to repel insects and pathogens and some are to help them avoid infections.

Regardless of how they are produced, essential oils can be used through different means: topically, through ingestion and through inhalation. They are fast acting and can infiltrate in the bloodstream easily. Every type of oil can also target a specific area or tissue in the body – this is true in both dogs and humans.

Essential oil compounds are also highly potent. This means that even a small amount could have tremendous effects on the body. One example is how even just a few drops of lavender oil can be used to calm dogs or make them sleepy when travelling.

A Brief History

The use of essential oils for medical purposes has its roots in ancient Egypt. At around the same period, the Chinese and Indians were also working on extracting plant materials in order to identify healing compounds. The knowledge about essential oils garnered from ancient Egypt was soon adopted by the Greeks – the "Father of Medicine" Hippocrates lead the way when it came to the discovery of holistic therapies. The process of developing essential oils continued, throughout the fall of the Roman Empire, through the work of the Persian doctor, Avicenna.

In Europe, essential oils were used to hide bad odors and even cure infections of fungal, viral and bacterial natures. Monks became educated in using oils and herbs for various treatments. The Renaissance period paved the way for Paracelsus, a renowned physician, to revive the movement towards natural and holistic therapies in an attempt to treat leprosy.

The popularity of essential oils in modern times was rekindled when a French perfumer named Gattefosse accidentally discovered that Lavender oil could effectively heal burns. Lavender oil was also used during the World War II to cure wounded soldiers. Further research into these oils continued and resulting in the finding and categorizing of the properties of essential oils. The researchers did not only center on the use of essential oils for the benefit of humans though - there were also researchers who dealt with "ethobotany" or the veterinary use of essential oils – this book will talk about that aspect.

If you love your dog, and want to improve its health and lifespan, learning about the benefits of essential oils and how they can be safely applied, is the only way forward.

Common Essential Oils

There are lots of oils that can be used to treat various dog ailments. That said, it is still a good idea to consult your veterinarian about the essential oils you are using, or would like to use, on your pet. Always make sure to get the vet involved in your decision, especially if they too are treating your dog.

To help you out, here are some of the safest essential oils for use on dogs:

Cardamom

This oil could help treat conditions like nausea, coughs, colic and heartburn. It also fights infection and urinary problems in dogs.

Lavender

This is the most popular essential oil among essential oil users. It can be used in diluted or undiluted form. It can aid in treating burns, skin irritation, wounds, ticks and flea in dogs and even anxiety and insomnia. This is highly recommended and should be part of every kit.

Bergamot

This soothing oil comes with outstanding anti-fungal properties. It is great for ear infections caused by the overgrowth of bacteria or yeast. Just a warning: photo-sensitization is a side effect. Avoid sun exposure after use.

Cedarwood

It fights infection and stimulates the circulation making it effective for dermatitis. It also helps in repelling ticks and fleas.

Serenity

It is a safe and gentle oil used to relieve inflammation – it is suitable for minor burns, allergic reactions and skin irritation.

Sweet Jasmine

It deodorizes, calms the nerves and repels fleas. It can make your pet sensitive to sunlight, so use with caution. It should also be noted that the oil labelled Sweet Jasmine in the store is undoubtedly adulterated with a different oil - Jasmine Absolute is extremely expensive.

Peppermint

Repels insects, stimulates circulation and relieves strains, sprains and arthritis in dogs. It can be blended with ginger and rubbed on the tummy to cure motion-sickness. Another must have!

Ginger

Non-irritating and non-toxic, just use it in minute amounts. Good for digestion, motion sickness and pain associated with sprains, strains and arthritis.

Myrrh

Great for skin problems and ear infections brought about by allergies due to its potent anti-bacterial properties.

Eucalyptus

It works as an expectorant, anti-inflammatory and anti-viral, popularly used to treat chest congestion. It also works well against fleas.

Marjoram

It offers a calming effect along with its strong anti-septic properties. It also helps in calming the nerves. Good for a lot of common ailments in dogs, such as wounds, skin infection and insect infestation.

Carrot Seed

It helps boosts energy, fight infection and improve circulation. It is ideal for flaky, dry and highly sensitive skin vulnerable to infection. This oil works wonders by promoting build-up of new tissues and skin cells making it effective in healing scars.

Animals respond to essential oils very well. With the right knowledge and ample care, these essential oils can be utilized for almost any ailment – from ticks and fleas infestation to skin irritations, infections and more.

Chapter 2: Benefits of Using Essential Oil for your Pets

Essential oils are, simply, the organic components from plants that are extracted and refined to preserve the natural curative properties of the plant. Tons of laboratory experiments have led the way to the discovery of the various curative benefits. Interestingly, the use of essential oils for therapeutic and healing purposes in animals has increased significantly over time.

The big question now is: Are they really more safe and effective than synthetic medications for animals?

At this point, you may have made yourself familiar with the different essential oils and how these can help make your beloved pet feel healthier and better. These oils can be used for almost all kinds of animals, especially your canine friend. This chapter will deal with the superb benefits that pets can get from the use of essential ails as a curative strategy.

Let's take a closer look at these gains:

Convenience and Ease

The great thing with essential oils is that they are so easy to use – convenience is paramount to pet owners. You can choose to allow it to diffuse around your home or apply it directly to the affected area on your pet. It takes is just a few seconds of your time to apply the treatment.

In some cases, the oils can be administered in their pure form, in most cases, however, you need to dilute the oils. Don't panic - diluting these oils is pretty easy and you will not be confused at all. It's as easy as 1-2-3.

Safety

Essential oils are S-A-F-E. Yes, because they are all natural, there is no need to be anxious where they came from or whether they are dangerous. The potential benefits do outweigh any possible risks.

Besides which, compared to commercially prepared pharmaceuticals for animals that exist on the market, these oils are completely harmless. The trick is getting the right dosage, using high quality oils and in making sure that you apply the oils properly.

Fast-Action

Essential oils work almost instantly in most cases. For instance, some pet owners diffuse oils to improve their pets' health and overall condition. This involves diffusing oil right into the air, in a closed space within the home – this is known as aromatherapy. Animals respond to the aromatic scent in as fast as 1 to 3 seconds. This is why inhalation is the most common method of administering essential oils.

If applied topically, these oils are expected to be absorbed into the skin almost immediately. So, your pets will experience the positive effects soon after you administer the oil. Pets who require first aid will definitely benefit from essential oils.

Anti-Oxidant Properties

Humans need a great deal of anti-oxidants to get rid of free radicals in the body. Well, your pets do too! The good thing is that essential oils are rich in anti-oxidants. Thus, your pets will definitely benefit as these elements work at eliminating the harmful toxins in their bodies too.

What are the effects? Well, there is a smaller chance that your pet will become ill due to an enhanced immune system. It also energizes the body keeping performance at optimal levels.

Good for the Tummy

Animals experience distress in the stomach in much the same way as you do at times. Luckily, you don't have to resort immediately to advanced pharmaceuticals to soothe your pet's digestion.

Essential oils, like peppermint and ginger can help when there is something wrong with your pet's tummy – tummy ailments are common in dogs. At times like these, essential oils can soothe the upset and get the digestive tract running smoothly again.

Pain Relief

Pets suffer the effects of aging just as much as we do. Animals are also prone to a variety of muscle and joint problems that can cause extreme pain when not treated properly.

Some of these conditions include arthritis, sprains, strains and displaced bones. These conditions can cause a great deal of pain, making movement almost impossible. Fortunately, a massage using essential oils with analgesic properties, like chamomile, will alleviate inflammation and pain keeping your pet strong and mobile.

Flea and Tick Protection

Flea and ticks are one of the top enemies of your pets – especially when it comes to dogs and cats. Pets are particularly vulnerable when they are unhealthy and weak. Common over the counter products used to counter ticks and fleas, such as sprays, collars and topical drops could cause tremors, breathing problems, vomiting and even nerve damage. In addition, drugs can damage the vital organs – kidneys and liver.

Generally, ticks and fleas love it when the pet's immune system is compromised. So, the best way to prevent the problem is to boost immune system; thus, reducing vulnerability to these blood suckers. Essential oils, like cedarwood can be helpful in this instance.

Enhanced Health

Apart from the ailments mentioned above, there are many other health problems that can be cured using essential oils. If your pet is suffering from a specific ailment, one that you think can be dealt with using essential oils, it is a good idea to discuss the matter with an experienced holistic veterinarian. They can present you with what options, in terms of essential oils, will be the safest and best for your beloved pet.

These are just some of the primary benefits that your pet will experience when provided with the right treatment using essential oils. There are many other secondary benefits that are not talked about here – the exact results will depend on what kind of oil you are going to be using. It will help to explore the different types of essential oils obtainable to see which will work best for your pet.

Chapter 3: Oil Application Techniques for Dogs

As an animal lover, it is your responsibility to learn what is best for your pets. This applies to almost everything, including the use of essential oils in the treatment of health ailments. So, you should seek out all vital information about the use of oils – usage, dosage, administration techniques and safety precautions.

If you are thinking of using oils for your dogs, this chapter will teach you all the basic guidelines when it comes to safety issues of using oils to treat your canine friend.

Aromatherapy for Dogs

Using essential oils to treat different health problems in dogs is referred to as "aromatherapy". Some of these health issues range from skin irritations, nose and ear infections to tick and flea infestation and even agitation. This form of alternative treatment is becoming popular due to its safety and effectiveness.

However, it is important to realize that using essential oils is not just about deodorizing your dog. As mentioned in the earlier chapters, essential oils have strong medicinal properties and can be really effective in healing a wide range of health issues in dogs. In addition, these essential oils can be mixed up together for synergistic effects.

How these oils will work depend on how you use them. So, it is best to learn how to apply the treatment properly to get the best effects possible.

Application Techniques

Basically, essential oils can be applied to your dogs in three ways:

Inhalation and Diffusion

Aromatherapy can be implemented through diffusion or inhalation. In this process, you will need a diffuser. The diffuser heats up the oils and, as they evaporate, their aroma is inhaled by your dog. Ideally you should allow the diffuser to run for around 30 to 45 minutes, so your dog gets the best benefits.

How often should you do this?

Inhalation treatment with essential oils should be done twice a day over the period of a week. Positive results can be expected within this time frame.

Ingestion

Essential oils should never be taken internally unless under the direct supervision of an holistic vet. Even then, taking the oils internally is really a last resort - The oils are highly concentrated and can even be toxic if to much is ingested.

Topical

This is the most common application technique, and offers the highest benefit since the oil is directly applied to the affected area. With this, the oil gets absorbed in the skin to the small capillaries, and then into the bloodstream.

Topical application is possible through massage or sprays or the addition of the oils to ointments, creams, shampoos and conditioners. You may apply the oils to the toe pads, ears, and spine or directly to the wound and almost anywhere except the genitals, anal area, nose and eyes. All you need to do is to rub the oil or preparation to your palm and apply to the affected part. You may also use applicators like wooden sticks or tongue depressor with gauze pads. If treating an open sore, you can drop the blend directly into it.

Take note: the essential oils require dilution prior to use. Some of the carrier oils you may use may include, but are not limited to, the following: jojoba oil, olive oil, coconut oil and sweet almond oil.

Safety Precautions

You definitely don't want to cause harm to your buddy, so here are some measures to take to safely apply essential oils to dogs:

Dilution

The only two essential oils that are suitable to be use neat are Lavender and Tea Tree oil. Every other oil must be diluted before use. Because the oils are so concentrated, even the diluted blend is still very strong.

You need to consider the size of the dog when considering what dilution to use. The essential oils should form no more than 0.5% to 1% of the overall mixture. For smaller dogs, this relates to 3 drops for every 30ml of oil. For larger dogs, this relates to 6 drops for every 30ml.

It is good practice to use the lowest concentration first and to only increase this concentration should it be absolutely necessary. When it comes to more fragile dogs, puppies or dogs with compromised immune system, you need to use a lower concentration.

Pregnant Dogs

Be extra careful if your dog is pregnant – you should rather avoid using any essential oils in this case. There are oils that are stimulating in nature and may cause premature delivery and other complications on expecting dogs. Some of the essential oils to avoid include the following:

- Tea tree oil

- Niaouli

- Eucalyptus

- Peppermint

- Rosemary

To avoid possible problems, discuss the matter with a holistic vet before beginning treatment of pregnant dogs.

Allergic Reactions

Your dog may lick the area where you apply the essential oils. This is a common occurrence and normally does not lead to problems. That said, you do need to ensure that your pet will not have any negative or allergic reaction. Just in case, allow the skin to absorb the oils and then wipe the affected spot with a wet cloth dipped in a mild soap.

If your dog is suffering negative effects from the ingestion of essential oils, go to the vet right away. These include the following: diarrhea, vomiting, extreme weakness, tremors, seizures and excessive salivation.

Breathing Problems

If you observe breathing problems or coughing due to the scent of the essential oil, get your dog out of the room and get in touch with the vet if symptoms continue. It is also not a good practice to force the aroma onto your dog through the use of a muzzle mask or head gear - the experience should be pleasant for your dog.

Eye Contact

Essential oils should not be placed into or near the eyes, nose and genitals. If you accidentally put oil to these areas, flushing with sterile saline or water is recommended. You may also use milk to aid in the flushing and neutralizing of any oil residue.

Overall, you should be very cautious when applying essential oils. Nine times out of ten you should adopt a "less is more" approach. Oils should not be over-utilized either, as this will decrease their effectiveness when they are really needed. Just think this way:" when you are in doubt, don't administer".

Chapter 4: Therapeutic Oil Uses for Dogs

The therapeutic use of essential oils is a cost-effective and wonderful way to help yourself and your dog face different health conditions. Dogs and humans alike benefit from these oils, due to their similarities in physiological make up. Dogs are extremely responsive and sensitive to the aroma and healing wonders of these oils making aromatherapy a great alternative to conventional treatment options.

This section will detail the common therapeutic uses of essential oils and how they can be used effectively to achieve healing. You will learn how to reduce your dog's anxiety, change his moods and help him live a stress-free life.

Is Your Dog Stressed?

It is interesting to know that animals get stressed too. Yes, it's a fact. As a loving owner, you have to take any measures that you can to make sure that this stress is minimized. Now, how do you know if your dog is facing some issues? Here are the top reasons why your dog could be suffering from anxiety and stress:

Separation

Dogs are like toddlers as they also feel anxious when separated from their parents. They may feel sad if you travel a lot or when you spend long hours at work. In turn, they will be more moody and clingy when you are at home. And. worse still, they are likely to feel nervous tension every time you go away.

New Environment

Some dogs find it hard to adjust to a new environment. The usual symptoms include hiding in the bathroom rather than in their dog house, loss of appetite and sensitivity to even the smallest noises. If you have you moved into a new house, and you see that your dog has any of these symptoms, think about using essential oils to calm your dogs.

Lack of Attention

Dogs are attention seekers and they need to feel that they are loved by their owners. They may create trouble when you do not pay much attention to them. So, aside from showing a bit of care and love, another good way to deal with anxiety and stress in dogs is to use essential oils.

What Essential Oils to Use

these reasons are just the tip of the iceberg when it comes to the causes of anxiety and stress in dogs. Just think of it this way: if something stresses you out, there is a good chance that it is having an effect on your best friend as well. If you want to help your dog cope, here are the best essential oils that you can use:

· Chamomile

· Lavender

· Lemon

· Sweet Marjoram

· Clary Sage

How do you use these?

You can either apply these oils topically or diffuse them into the air. If you choose to apply topically, you have to mix the essential oils into a carrier oil or you risk burning your dog's skin. If you have a diffuser at home, aromatherapy is really great option.

Just put the right amount in the diffuser and turn it on for around 30 minutes each day. Do this for seven days straight and you will see a big improvement in your dog's mood, energy and attitude.

Try this proven aromatherapy recipe – it works by calming dogs who are experiencing noise anxiety, separation anxiety or fear of certain people, things or places.

With this, you will need the following:

- 15 ml sweet almond or olive oil

- 5 drops lavender

- 4 drops sweet marjoram

- 3 drops clary sage

- 2 drops valerian

All you need to do is to mix the ingredients together and mix well. For topical application, put a few drops of the solution on your palm and rub the oil between your palms. Then, massage into areas like the armpits, toe spaces, outer ear edges and the thighs.

You can come up with other blends of essential oils to help your dog out when you feel that something is not quite right with his overall state. Just make sure that all the oils that you are using are therapeutic grade oils that are pure and unadulterated.

Chapter 5: Insect Repellent Oil Uses for Dogs

Essential oils are highly recommended for repelling insects and parasites on your dog. These oils, when combined with water, witch hazel or carrier oils and misted onto the dog or mixed with shampoo can help not only to deter insects, but also to enhance the immune system and soothe the skin. There are a lot of advantages to using essential oils on your dogs.

Protect Your Dog

The presence of insects or any form of bugs and parasites on your dog serve as an indicator of poor health. Yes, that's right. These insects are attracted to unhealthy dogs with damaged immune system. The perfect solution to this is to make your pet less susceptible through the use of essential oils.

Though tons of commercially available products can be used to repel insects on dogs, these poses direct risks to your pet. For instance, dog shampoos, sprays, collars and medications used to drive away insects could potentially cause a wide array of health problems like tremors, mouth sores, breathing problems and worst, liver and kidney damage.

With essential oils, your dog will get a host of other benefits,on top of the eradication of parasites. These oils also aid in soothing the skin, healing the wounds caused by insect bites and boosting the immune system. So, say goodbye to ill health in your dog with the help of essential oils and get rid of harmful, synthetic chemicals forever.

The Role of Essential Oils

Most plants manufacture essential oils to aid in their survival and to repel insects. The amazing thing is, these oils can also be used to protect humans and animals. Your dog can also benefit greatly from the natural oils as these work effectively in strengthening the immune system and, through the eradication of bugs, caring for your dog's coat as well.

Thanks to Mother Nature, repelling insects for your dog's sake can be achieved in a safe, easy and natural manner. Here are a few essential oils you may use:

Citronella

Citronella does not only work with mosquitoes, it can also repel ticks, fleas and black flies. It is non-toxic and all natural and serves as an excellent alternative to chemical repellents. Combine it with other essential oils like cedarwood to achieve the best benefits.

Lavender

It is not only known for its sweet smell, it can also be used to deter ticks and other insects and also as prevent insect eggs from hatching.

Peppermint

Peppermint known for its rich menthol content. It can be used to repel ticks and fleas, and even mice and spiders.

Lemongrass

Its lovely citrus scent helps to deter ticks and fleas. It will also boost immunity. It should be used in a very diluted format as it can irritate the skin. Be wary of cheap imitations as well.

Cedarwood

This highly aromatic oil contains a pheromone that can disrupt the mental capacity of insects and help to deter them at the same time.

Juniper

It repels insects, cleanses and detoxifies the body while protecting the kidneys. It is safe and mild on your dog's skin as well, as long as properly diluted.

Basic Usage Instructions

How do you use essential oils to repel insects? Well, it's easy. Just get a spray bottle and fill it with 500ml of water, then put 15 drops or so of the essential oil of your choice. Mist your dog everyday, taking care not to get any into his eyes or nose, and spray on the doorways and bedding as well.

Dogs with allergies caused by these bugs could also get immediate relief while you are driving the insects away from the environment as well. If the insects tend to localize in the ears, you must cover your dog's eyes using your hand and spray the oil around the ear. Doing this will heal insect bites and repel insects.

For longer protection, you may put 2-3 drops of the oil on your dog's cotton collar. The scent can be renewed after a few days to sustain the effects. Or, you may just put some oil in your palms, rub them together and apply on your dog's skin and coat - beginning at the neck all the way to the tail and the legs.

Chapter 6: Deodorizing Oil Recipes for Dogs

Walking inside your home after a long day of work or shopping, and encountering your stinky best friend is not the greatest fun. It's hard, we love our dogs but they have a very different idea of what smells good than we do and sometimes they roll in the worst stuff. They are also more than happy to spread around that smell too.

So, you may want to mull over using deodorizing essential oils to fight the bad smell.

Essential oils work just fine whether you are looking for a product that you can use to bathe your dog in order to restore that "new puppy smell" or just looking for a quick fix. In fact, you can also use essential oils recipes to get rid of horrible dog smells around the house.

Here are some of the best recipes to keep your buddy smell clean and fresh without the aid of harsh chemicals:

Recipe#1: Bad Smell No More Shampoo

This DIY shampoo for dogs works effectively in deodorizing and providing moisture to dry skin.

- 250ml of water

- 15 ml of castile soap

- 5 drops lavender

- 3 drops peppermint

- 3 drops purification

- 2 drops cedarwood

- 2 drops citronella (optional for repelling fleas)

Combine all ingredients in a glass bottle or dispenser. It may appear watery, but you should use it like a regular dog shampoo. This solution does not lather that much but it is mild and effective. Your dog will smell good and fresh for days!

Recipe #2: Spray the Odor Away

This is a deodorizing spray recipe, which is very useful when you need a quick fix for your dog's stinky odor. This is perfect after a walk outside.

- 150 ml water

- 15 drops purification oil

- 5 drops lavender oil

- A dash of salt

In a spray bottle, put in the salt and then add all the essential oils. Stir gently and then add the water. This method of preparation aids in the even distribution of oils n the water.

To use, spray the mixture onto your dog.

Recipe#3: Essential Oil Spritz

This recipe can get rid of that bad smell without the need to bath your dog. It is also a good for treatment for their bedding and the areas where your dog spends most of his time.

- 240ml of water

- 10 drops purification oil

- 5 drops peppermint

Mix all the ingredients in a spray bottle and shake well. Spray directly onto your dog's coat. The bad smell will lift almost immediately. You may also spray the doorways, mats, bedding and other areas in your home.

Recipe#4: Deodorizing Dog Collar

You can use this recipe to create your own version of deodorizing dog collar.

- 80ml of water

- 3 drops lavender

- 3 drops purification

- 2 drops citronella

- 2 drops peppermint

Combine all ingredients in a bowl. Soak the dog collar in the mixture. Make sure to use this blend for collars made of cloth material since essential oils can destroy plastic. Collars that are made of natural fibers also work fine.

Leave it to dry completely before putting it on your dog. This is really important as natural fibers and cotton may shrink as they dry. Voila! You do not only get to deodorize your dog, you also help him drive away insects. Soak the collar every two weeks for the best results.

As you can see, it is easy to create your own deodorizing blends using essential oils. Just make sure that you use only certified and pure oils in treating your dog.

Chapter 7: Ear Care Oil Recipes for Dogs

Ear problems are not rare to dogs and may be caused by yeast or bacterial infection. Several factors are known to contribute to ear ailments, such as ear infestation, trapped water, air or foreign object inside the ear. In some cases, the overgrowth of microorganisms may also be related to a poor immune system and allergies.

Since the ear canals of dogs align horizontally from its opening, extracting trapped elements inside can be extremely difficult and this makes dogs prone to ear infections. Other activities that cause ear infections include excessive swimming or bathing and incorrect cleaning methods.

Moreover, a diet rich in soy, corn and other grains, found in many dog foods, can promote yeast infection as well as damage the immune system.

How can you tell if your dog has ear infection? Here are the most common symptoms:

- Redness
- Swelling
- Hair loss
- Balance problems
- Foul ear odor
- Excessive ear scratching
- Hearing loss
- Shaking of head
- Crusting near the ear
- Yellow bloody discharge

In traditional veterinary practice, topical medications, oral antibiotics and surgery, in the worst cases, are used to treat ear infections. The use of essential oils has been increasing in popularity due to its efficacy. The good thing with this form of alternative treatment is, you can apply it in the comforts of your own home at less expense.

The beauty in using essential oils to treat ear disorders is that you can make your own. There are tons of recipes that you can come up with. Here is a selection of the best of these:

Recipe#1: 5-Oil Ear Spray

This recipe makes use of 5 types of essential oil. To make this ear spray, you just need to combine the following in a 100ml spray bottle made of glass:

- 10 drops basil

- 10 drops lavender

- 10 drops arborvitae

- 10 drops frankincense

-10 drops geranium

- Coconut oil should fill 75% of the bottle

Shake the bottle prior to use. Spray once every week to treat ear infection in dogs or once per month to serve as a preventive measure if your dog is vulnerable to repeated ear infections.

Recipe#2: Soothing Ear Blend

This recipe is designed for severely infected or inflamed ear:

- 15 drops lavender oil

- 15 drops tea tree oil

- 100 ml of coconut oil

Mix all ingredients and keep in a clean glass bottle. A small amount should be applied to the ear using a cotton ball. Spread the oil onto the affected area in the ear to soothe the inflammation.

Recipe#3: Essential Oil Ear Cleanser

Infected ears require a great deal of cleaning. Though you may use soap and other products, why not opt for natural essential oil formulation that is safe and effective like this one?

- 15 drops lavender

- 10 drops tea tree oil

- 10 drops bergamot

- 100 ml of carrier oil or alcohol

Remember not to use products like mineral and baby oil as these could cause plugs in the pores and may lead to more problems.

To clean the ears, put a few drops of the solution to a cotton swab and use it to clean wax and dirt. Make sure you do not push the swab beyond the ear opening.

If ear wax builds up in your dog's ear canal, just apply 3-4 drops of the blend into the ear opening and rub the external ear. This may a little bit nasty and your nose may sense a foul smell. But this really helps in getting the wax out, so you can clean it right away.

There you go! Here are only some of the recipes you could try when caring for your dog with ear problems. When done correctly, expensive and more advanced treatments may no longer be required.

Chapter 8: Nose Care Oil Recipes for Dogs

Dogs are extremely curious creatures. They sniff just about everything, and get up to all sorts of mischief. This makes them more prone to scrapes, wounds, allergic reactions and other things that may harm them. You can help them get better faster through the use of essential oils.

Lavender oil, for instance, is absolutely great for treating burns, wounds and other skin conditions that you would normally treat with oral antibiotics and creams. In this section, you will learn about some of the most proven recipes using essential oils for your dog's nose care regimen. Whilst you would normally avoid using oils on your dog's nose, you have to take special action when he has hurt it.

Here are some essential oil recipes that you can make for your dog:

Recipe#1: 2-Oil Nose Blend for Dogs

- 5 drops of lemongrass

- 2 drops rosemary

- 60 ml of carrier oil

Combine all ingredients and either drop onto or massage into the affected area. This is good if your dog has hurt his nose. This blend hastens healing, cleanses and fights infection as well. Apply twice a day using a cotton ball or applicator.

Recipe#2: Breathe Easy Oil Blend

Sinus infection in dogs could often lead to nasal congestion making it hard for your dog to breathe. Here is a recipe that can help relieve this condition:

- 90ml carrier oil like coconut or sweet almond

- 5 drops myrhh

- 5 drops eucalyptus

- 5 drops ravens hare

Combine all ingredients and in dark glass container and shake thoroughly. To use, put a few drops on your palms and massage to your dog's chest and neck area. You may also apply some on a big handkerchief and tie it around the neck.

Another way to relieve congestion using this blend is to add 5 to 10 drops into your dog's sleeping area. Allow the dog to lie down on the ground and absorb the vaporizing oil to clear nose congestion.

Recipe#3: Itching Be Gone

You may see your dog scratching his nose almost non-stop. This may be a sign that your dog has an allergy. Use this recipe as remedy:

- 90ml olive oil

- 10 drops lavender

- 3 drops chamomile

- 3 drops geranium

- 1 drop niaouli

This creates a blend that you can use to relieve itching in the nasal area as well as other parts of the body. Put a few drops in a cotton ball and apply topically on affected areas. Just don't let the oil get inside your dog's nose. Do this twice daily to achieve optimum results.

Recipe#4: Nose Oil Wound Solution

Your dog's nose is prone to injuries like cuts, bruises, scrapes, insect bites. This blend is a great remedy for such injuries:

- 60 ml olive oil

- 5 drops lavender

- 3 drops sweet marjoram

- 3 drops niaouli

- 2 drops helichrysum

Combine all ingredients together and shake well. Apply on affected areas twice daily until it is healed.

Along with these recipes, you may also diffuse essential oils within your home as the aroma enters the body through the nose and targets illnesses from within. By doing so, you are doing a great favor for your dog and this small act can go a long way.

Chapter 9: Skin & Coat Oil Recipes for Dogs

Dogs love the outdoors and are thus prone to skin irritation brought about by being exposed to too much air and sunlight. They scratch and sniff and even roll over the place in order to alleviate the itching. Just like humans, their skin suffers from allergies, infection and inflammation too! These may be caused by the environment, infestation or an internal ailment.

An unhealthy coat usually accompanies skin problems. When the skin is not healthy, a health problem could be indicated and it will affect the health of your dog's coat. You can by a myriad of topical creams, oral medications, medicated shampoos and other synthetic products to deal with skin and coat issues in dogs if you want to. Are you going to be truly satisfied with the results though? Can you be sure that these commerial preparations are not bad for your dog?

There many alternatives to be sure, but using essential oils rates as one of the best. If you need some assistance when it comes to taking care of your dog's skin and fur, follow these incredible recipes:

Recipe#1: Skin Care Topical Blend

This recipe has been proven to be highly effective for skin itching and redness:

- 150ml carrier oil (sweet almond or olive oil)

- 5 drops chamomile

- 5 drops lavender

2 drops tea tree

2 drops frankincense

Combine all of the ingredients and place in a glass container. To use, apply 2-3 drops directly on the affected area in order to relieve itching. Apply twice a day or as often as necessary.

Recipe#2: 5 Drop Essential Oils Blend

Small cuts, minor eczema, bruises as well as cracked skin can be treated by using this great recipe:

- 150ml carrier oil of your choice

- 5 drops of patchouli

- 5 drops of myrrh

- 5 drops lavender

Mix all components together in a glass bottle and shake vigorously. Put 2-3 drops of this blend in a cotton ball or swab and apply to the affected area twice a day.

Recipe#3: Gentle Skin and Coat Oil Blend

You may use body rinses with essential oils to make your dog's coat and skin a lot healthier without having to use chemical agents. This recipe is super light and will not disturb your dog's sensitive nose.

- 500ml herbal tea like chamomile

- 10 drops peppermint

- 10 drops rosemary

- 5 drops eucalyptus

- 5 drops citronella

- 15ml apple cider vinegar

To prepare, just boil 500ml of water and pour it over the herbal tea. Leave it for 15 to 20 minutes or until the blend is lukewarm. Add the apple cider vinegar and dilute the solution with another 500 ml of water.

This blend can be used as the last rinse for your dog during bath time. You may also use a cloth soaked in the solution to cleanse your dog's face. Alternatively, spray it directly onto his coat. Apart from adding shine to the coat, it also helps in relieving skin inflammation and flaking.

Recipe#4: Allergy Buster

If your dog is prone to allergies, this easy recipe will definitely offer fast relief:

- 2 tablespoons of aloe gel

- 3 drops lavender oil

- 3 drops eucalyptus

- 2 drops helichrysum

Place the aloe vera gel in a glass container. Then, add in the essential oils. Stir and apply to the affected area using a cotton ball or swab. Apply 2-3 times a day to relieve skin allergies.

All of these recipes are safe for dogs. To ensure the highest level of safety, it is best to perform a patch test prior to full application. Also, observe your dog within 24 hours of administration and make sure you report to the vet should any untoward symptoms appear.

Chapter 10: Flea & Tick Oil Recipes for Dogs

Treating your dog for a tick and flea problem is easy when using essential oils. If you are on the hunt for natural remedies to deter these pests, this section is for you.

Almost all tick and flea products in the market contain toxic chemicals that can harm your dog's health and even cause death. Though these harsh components are needed to kill the ticks and fleas, these products are not highly recommended as they might not only be dangerous to your pet, but to YOU as well.

So, why not make the most of essential oils to repel insects and pests? These oils have aromatic smells that distracts the ticks and fleas hate.

With a bit of experimentation on these natural recipes, you will be able to create an awesome tick and flea home treatment regimen for your best buddy.

Recipe#1: Bye Fleas Blend

This recipe can be used to repel the fleas on your pet dog. You may add 250ml of organic shampoo as the base or 100ml of carrier oil if you want an oil-based formulation:

- 8 drops peppermint

- 5 drops lemon

- 5 drops clary sage

- 3 drops citronella

To use, apply a few drops of the solution to your dog's chest, neck, tail and legs. It is also advisable to put some of the blend onto your dog's collar, using material made of cotton or any other natural fiber. You may also use this like a regular dog shampoo if you choose to dilute it that way. Do it once a week and you will see a big difference.

Recipe#2: Tick and Flea Terminator

- 60ml carrier oil

- 3ml alcohol

- 3 drops lavender

- 3 drops cedarwood

- 2 drops citronella

- 2 drops thyme

Using a brush, run the blend throughout the coat and focus on areas where ticks and fleas usually attach – armpits, neck, head and ears.

You can also make a tick and flea deterring collar by soaking the collar in the blend. This will offer a month long protection. Re-soak as necessary.

Recipe#3: Spray the Pests Away

This recipe is an organic spray that you can use to get rid of ticks and fleas on your dog's fur:

- 240ml water

- 240ml apple cider vinegar

- 10ml sweet almond oil

- 10ml lemon oil or citronella

- 5ml garlic oil

Mix all ingredients together in a spray bottle and shake well. Spray throughout the coat, especially in areas where ticks and fleas tend to concentrate on. Do this treatment once a week.

Recipe#4: Daily Tick and Flea Spray

This is an essential oil spray that you can use daily to make your dog tick and flea free.

- 120ml water

- 6 drops purification oil

- 2 drops palo santo

- 2 drops castile soap

Put everything in a spray container and shake well. Spray to your dog's coat every day. This blend works really well.

These recipes are great and they are guaranteed to deliver favorable results. Just a tip: always use dark bottles made of glass as containers. Essential oils could wear away plastic and will degrade quickly if exposed to sunlight. Also, make it a habit to put labels on the bottle - you are not always going to remember what blend is in what bottle.

Chapter 11: The Best Online Resources for Essential oil for Dogs

Essential oils are truly God's gift. There are hundreds of oils out there and you can make an infinite number of blends to treat just about every condition you can imagine. Every oil and formulation gives you the chance to make changes in your life and that of your dog.

That said, you do need to know what you are doing before you start experimenting so it is a good idea to do more research on the matter before you start making your blends.

The great news is that there is a wealth of information online - using this book as a starting point, you can further your skills by visiting the following sites:

Essential Animals

Essential Animals offer natural solutions for dogs and other animals, including human beings. They help by promoting happier and healthier lives through the use of Mother Nature's remedies. They offer the best products, knowledge and inspiration if you are looking for information about holistic care for your dogs.

What they provide are natural, effective and safe options – like the use of essential oils. Visit their page: www.essentianimals.com and learn more about the natural treatment modalities for dogs through the blogs, courses and books available on their site. You may also join forums and get a chance to consult with experienced practitioners. They will be happy to answer your queries! Most importantly, they also sell quality and certified essential oils and other natural products that you can use for treating your dog.

Experience Essential

Experience Essential is a great option if you are looking for the best information resource about essential oils for dogs. This site aims to educate and inspire you to the use of natural treatment modalities for your canine buddy. You will not only find blogs, articles and general information pages , you will learn a lot! Just visit www.experience-essential-oils.com and have a look around.

You can also avail of oil purchasing tips and get access to the highest grade essential oils. Plus, you may also subscribe to training sessions, classes and seminars to boost your skills in using essential oils.

Amazon

Of course, don't forget that Amazon is always there to give you the information, product and motivation that you are searching for. Just go to www.amazon.com and look for informational products and essential oils to help you to put what you have learned into practice.

Conclusion

Thank you again for downloading this book!

I hope this book was able to help you learn more about the art of using essential oils, their history, benefits, therapeutic effects in dogs and how they work.

Your dog is your best friend and you don't want him to feel ill for a minute longer than necessary. Aromatherapy is the answer if you are searching for a natural alternative that offers safe, effective, natural and cost effective healing. Naturally the holistic veterinarian plays an important part in this process as well.

The next step is to implement what you have learned from this book in your day-to-day life. The essential oil recipes presented in this book are more than worth a try, they have been proven to help. All it takes is a few minutes of your time and a bit of effort.

Reap the benefits essential oils have to offer by taking action NOW! You are doing your dog a great favor if you do.

Finally, if you enjoyed this book, please take the time to share your thoughts and post a review on Amazon. I would really appreciate it!

Thank you and good luck!

Made in the USA
Columbia, SC
01 April 2019